# a *smile* increases your face value

Dedicated to those who measure
their net worth by the number of smiles
they bring to others.

Especially for:

*These quotations were collected
over a period of years,
and until now only shared
with a few close friends
and associates. All of the authors are
not known; however,
we wish to acknowledge them
wherever they may be.*

Cartoons by Pete Secker

Copyright © 1990, Great Quotations, Inc.

All rights reserved. No part of this publication may be reproduced, stored in a retrieval system, or transmitted in any form or by any means, electronic, mechanical, photocopying, recording or otherwise without the prior consent of Great Quotations, Inc.

ISBN: 1-56245-011-5

"*a smile* increases your face value"

# "In spite of the cost of living it's still popular."

Kathleen Norris

"a *smile* increases your face value"

# "I got the bill for my surgery. Now I know why those doctors were wearing masks."

James H. Barrie

"a *smile* increases your face value"

# "Better to remain silent and be thought a fool than to speak out and remove all doubt."

Abraham Lincoln

"a *smile* increases your face value"

"A banker is a fellow who lends you his umbrella when the sun is shining and wants it back the minute it begins to rain."

"*a smile* increases your face value"

"If you pick up a starving dog and make him prosperous, he will not bite you.

This is the principal difference between a dog and a man."

Mark Twain

"a *smile* increases your face value"

# "God must love the common man, he made so many of them."

Abraham Lincoln

"a *smile* increases your face value"

"Retirement is when a man who figured he'd go fishing seven times a week finds himself washing the dishes three times a day."

"a *smile* increases your face value"

"When a man steals your wife, there is no better revenge than to let him keep her."

Sacha Guitry

"a *smile* increases your face value"

# "If I had known I was going to live this long I would have taken better care of myself."

"a *smile* increases your face value"

"There is nothing so annoying as to have two people go right on talking when you're interrupting."

Mark Twain

"a *smile* increases your face value"

# "If you want to know how many friends you have, just buy a cottage on a lake."

"a *smile* increases your face value"

# "It is better to give than to lend, and it costs about the same."

Sir Philip Gibbs

"a *smile* increases your face value"

> "We can't all be heroes because somebody has to sit on the curb and clap as they go by."
>
> Will Rogers

> "**I** drink to make other people more interesting."
>
> George Jean Nathan

"a *smile* increases your face value"

# "It's not whether you win or lose— it's how you place the blame."

"a *smile* increases your face value"

# "Miracles are great, but they are so damned unpredictable."

Peter Drucker

"a *smile* increases your face value"

"The drive-in bank was established so that the real owner of a car could get to see it once in a while."

"a *smile* increases your face value"

# "Let us be thankful for the fools. But for them the rest of us could not succeed."

Mark Twain

"a *smile* increases your face value"

"Middle age is the time in life when it takes you longer to rest than it does to get tired."

"a *smile* increases your face value"

"The brain is a wonderful organ; it starts the minute you get up in the morning and does not stop until you get to the office."

Robert Frost

"a *smile* increases your face value"

# "Guests, like fish, begin to smell after three days."

Benjamin Franklin

"a *smile* increases your face value"

# "Don't be humble: you're not that great."

Golda Meir

"a *smile* increases your face value"

# "Anyone can win, unless there happens to be a second entry."

George Ade

"a *smile* increases your face value"

"You can always tell a real friend; when you've made a fool of yourself he doesn't feel you've done a permanent job."

Lawrence J. Peter

"a *smile* increases your face value"

"Always borrow from a pessimist— he never expects it back."

"a *smile* increases your face value"

# "Even if you're on the right track, you'll get run over if you just sit there."

Will Rogers

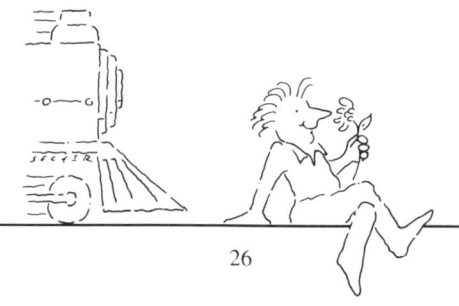

"a *smile* increases your face value"

"Blessed are the young, for they shall inherit the national debt."

"a *smile* increases your face value"

# "Advertising may be described as the science of arresting human intelligence long enough to get money from it."

"a *smile* increases your face value"

# "The closest to perfection a person ever comes is when they fill out a job application."

Stanley J. Randall

"a *smile* increases your face value"

"Before you borrow money from a friend, decide which you need more."

"a *smile* increases your face value"

"The person who marries for money usually earns every penny of it."

"a *smile* increases your face value"

# "Happiness is a positive cash flow."

Fred Adler

"a *smile* increases your face value"

"A jury should decide a case the minute they are shown it, before the lawyers have had a chance to mislead 'em."

Will Rogers

"a *smile* increases your face value"

"Laugh and the world laughs with you, snore and you sleep alone."

Anthony Burgess

"a *smile* increases your face value"

"Love is the answer; but while you are waiting for the answer, sex raises some pretty good questions."

Woody Allen

"a *smile* increases your face value"

---

"If at first you don't succeed, try, try again…then give up. There's no use being a damn fool about it."

W.C. Fields

"a *smile* increases your face value"

"Some who are not paid what they are worth ought to be glad."

"a *smile* increases your face value"

"When I was a boy of fourteen, my father was so ignorant I could hardly stand to have the old man around. But when I got to be twenty-one I was astonished at how much the old man had learned in seven years."

Mark Twain

"a *smile* increases your face value"

# "Three may keep a secret, if two of them are dead."

Benjamin Franklin

"a *smile* increases your face value"

"A chip on the shoulder is often a piece of wood that has fallen from the head."

"a *smile* increases your face value"

# "The two hardest things to handle in life are failure and success."

"a *smile* increases your face value"

"Ninety-eight percent of the adults in this country are decent, hard-working, honest Americans. It's the other lousy two percent that get all the publicity. But then we elected them."

Lily Tomlin

"a *smile* increases your face value"

"Some people are like a callus; they always show up when the work is finished."

"a *smile* increases your face value"

> "Money won't buy happiness, but it will pay the salaries of a large research staff to study the problem."
>
> Bill Vaughan

"a *smile* increases your face value"

# "Only two groups of people fall for flattery–men and women."

"a *smile* increases your face value"

"A nickel goes a long way now. You can carry it around for days without finding a thing it will buy."

"a *smile* increases your face value"

"Suppose you were an idiot and suppose you were a member of Congress.
But I repeat myself."

Mark Twain

"a *smile* increases your face value"

"When opportunity knocks, some people are in the backyard looking for four-leaf clovers."

"a *smile* increases your face value"

"**A**ll you need to grow fine, vigorous grass is a crack in your sidewalk."

Will Rogers

"a *smile* increases your face value"

# "Diplomacy:

# Thinking twice before saying nothing."

"a *smile* increases your face value"

# "A man can't be too careful in the choice of his enemies."

Oscar Wilde

"a *smile* increases your face value"

# "I don't make jokes. I just watch the government and report the facts."

Will Rogers

"a *smile* increases your face value"

"All husbands are alike, but they have different faces so you can tell them apart."

Anonymous

"a *smile* increases your face value"

# "Always forgive your enemies— nothing annoys them so much."

Oscar Wilde

"a *smile* increases your face value"

"If you get up early, work late, and pay your taxes, you will get ahead— if you win the lotto!"

"a *smile* increases your face value"

"Lead your life so you wouldn't be ashamed to sell the family parrot to the town gossip."

"The only fool bigger than the person who knows it all is the person who argues with him."

"a *smile* increases your face value"

# "It is ill-mannered to silence a fool, and cruelty to let him go on."

Benjamin Franklin

"a *smile* increases your face value"

"I've had a wonderful evening," said Groucho Marx after a very dull party, "but this wasn't it."

"**I**f all the economists in the world were laid end to end, it would probably be a good thing."

"a *smile* increases your face value"

"When the well's dry, we know the worth of water."

*"a smile increases your face value"*

> "He that scatters thorns, let him not go barefoot."

"a *smile* increases your face value"

# "One nice thing about egotists:

# They don't talk about other people."

"a *smile* increases your face value"

# "Love your enemies, for they tell you your faults."

*"a smile increases your face value"*

---

# "Income tax has made more liars out of the American people than golf has."

Will Rogers

"**You** have only to mumble a few words in church to get married and a few words in your sleep to get divorced."

"a *smile* increases your face value"

# "After all is said and done, more is said than done."

"a *smile* increases your face value"

# "I don't jog. If I die, I want to be sick."

Abe Lemons

*"a smile increases your face value"*

---

"There are two times when a man doesn't understand a woman—before marriage and after marriage."

"a *smile* increases your face value"

# "If you tell the truth, you don't have to remember anything."

Mark Twain

"a *smile* increases your face value"

"When you have got an elephant by the hind legs and he is trying to run away, it is best to let him run."

Abraham Lincoln

"a *smile* increases your face value"

"Some people don't have much to say, but you have to listen a long time to find it out."

"a *smile* increases your face value"

# "Forgive your enemies, but never forget their names."

John F. Kennedy

*"a smile increases your face value"*

"Vacation—
The period when
those rainy days
for which a
person saves,
usually arrive."

"a *smile* increases your face value"

> "A jury consists of twelve persons chosen to decide who has the better lawyer."
>
> Robert Frost

"a *smile* increases your face value"

# Murphy's law:

# "If anything can go wrong, it will."

"a *smile* increases your face value"

# O'Toole's commentary on Murphy's law:

# "Murphy was an optimist."

## *Other Great Quotations Books:*

- The Book of Proverbs
- Aged to Perfection
- Retirement
- Love on Your Wedding Day
- Thinking of You
- The Unofficial Executive Survival Guide
- Inspirations
- Sports Poop
- Over the Hill
- Golf Humor
- Happy Birthday to the Golfer
- Stress
- Cat Tales
- The Unofficial Christmas Survival Guide
- The Unofficial Survival Guide To Parenthood
- A Smile Increases Your Face Value
- Keys to Happiness
- Things You'll Learn...
- Teachers Inspirations
- Boyfriends Live Longer than...
- Worms of Wisdom
- Our Life Together
- Thoughts from the Heart
- An Apple a Day
- The Joy of Family
- What to Tell Your Children
- Proverbs Vol. II
- A Friend is a Present
- Books are Better in Bed than Men

GREAT QUOTATIONS, INC.
1967 Quincy Ct. • Glendale Heights, IL 60139

**TOLL FREE: 800-354-4889** (outside Illinois)
(708) 582-2800
PRINTED IN HONG KONG